W9-ANB-149

India

by Sarah E. De Capua

Content Adviser: Mark Liechty, Ph.D.,
Assistant Professor, Departments of History and Anthropology,
University of Illinois at Chicago

Reading Adviser: Dr. Linda D. Labbo,
Department of Reading Education, College of Education,
The University of Georgia

COMPASS POINT BOOKS

Minneapolis, Minnesota

FIRST REPORTS

Compass Point Books
3109 West 50th Street, #115
Minneapolis, MN 55410

Visit Compass Point Books on the Internet at *www.compasspointbooks.com*
or e-mail your request to *custserv@compasspointbooks.com*

Cover: Taj Mahal reflected in pool

Photographs ©: Brian A. Vikander/Corbis, cover, 9; Nigel J. Dennis/Gallo Images/Corbis, 4; Fatima
Martins/Corbis, 6; Flat Earth, 7, 32–33; Gary Milburn/Tom Stack & Associates, 8; Hulton/Archive by
Getty Images, 11, 12, 13, 35; John Elk III, 14–15, 31, 41 (left), 42–43; Doranne Jacobson, 16–17, 18, 21,
22, 30, 39; Inga Spence/Visuals Unlimited, 19; Charles Preitner/Visuals Unlimited, 20, 40; Catherine
Karnow/Corbis, 23; Jayanta Shaw/Reuters/Getty Images, 24, 47; Ami Vitale/Getty Images, 25; Sondeep
Shankar/Getty Images, 26; Pablo Bartholomew/Getty Images, 27; V. Muthuraman/Visuals Unlimited, 28,
29, 38; Graeme Goldin/Cordaiy Photo Library/Corbis, 36; Jeremy Horner/Corbis, 37; AFP/Corbis, 41
(right); Ron Wise, 45 (bottom).

Editors: E. Russell Primm, Emily J. Dolbear, and Patricia Stockland
Photo Researcher: Svetlana Zhurkina
Photo Selector: Linda S. Koutris
Designer/Page Production: Bradfordesign, Inc./Biner Design
Cartographer: XNR Productions, Inc.

Library of Congress Cataloging-in-Publication Data
De Capua, Sarah.
    India / by Sarah De Capua.
        p. cm. — (First reports)
    Summary: Introduces the geography, history, culture, and people of India, a large country in southern
Asia. Includes bibliographical references and index.
    ISBN 0-7565-0424-4 (hardcover)
    1. India—Juvenile literature. [1. India.] I. Title. II. Series.
    DS407 .D4 2003
954—dc21   2002009926

Table of Contents

"Namaste!" 4

Land and Weather 7

History of India 10

Made in India 16

Life in India 18

Festivals and Holidays 24

Arts and Literature 28

Indian Food 36

Indian Clothing 39

India Today 42

Glossary 44

Did You Know? 44

At a Glance 45

Important Dates 46

Want to Know More? 47

Index 48

*NOTE: In this book, words that are defined in the glossary are in **bold** the first time they appear in the text.*

"Namaste!"

▲ India has many different kinds of animals, including its national bird, the peacock.

Do you know how people say "hello" in India? They say *"Namaste!"* It is a Hindi greeting.

India is a country in southern Asia. India touches six countries. Pakistan lies to the northwest. China,

▲ Map of India

Nepal, and Bhutan are to the north. Bangladesh and
Myanmar are to the east. The southern part of India is
a **peninsula.** It sticks out into the ocean.

Three bodies of water wash up on India's shores. The Bay of Bengal lies to the east. The Indian Ocean is to the south. The Arabian Sea is west of the country.

More than one billion people live in India. That is more than any other country in the world except China.

New Delhi is the capital of India. This is where India's central government is located. The largest city in India is Mumbai. Mumbai was once known as Bombay. Other major cities include Calcutta and Varanasi.

▲ *Varanasi is one of India's major cities.*

Land and Weather

▲ *Part of the Himalaya Mountain range is in northern India.*

India has three main regions. The Himalaya Mountains form the northern border of India. Large, flat areas of land called plains lie at the foot of the mountains. The peninsula is in the south.

In the mountains, winters are very cold. It snows often. Summers are warm and dry.

To the south of the Himalayas lies the North Indian Plain. The Ganges (GAN-geez), Yamuna (yah-MUH-nah), and Brahmaputra (BRAH-ma-POO-tra) Rivers flow in the eastern part of the plain. These rivers make the area good for farming. Most of the people in India live there and farm the land for a living. In the Ganges River valley, winters are cool and dry.

▲ *Farmers in India use river water for farming.*

Summers are very hot until the annual heavy rains come. These welcome rains are known as monsoons. The farmers need them to water their crops.

In the south-western part of the North Indian Plain is the Thar Desert. It extends into the country of Pakistan.

The weather in India's peninsula is warmer and wetter than it is in the north. Some coastal areas get nearly 36 feet (11 meters) of rain each year!

◀ *The Thar Desert extends from India to Pakistan.*

History of India

The first cities and towns in the world appeared around 2500 B.C. in what is now northwest India. Around 1500 B.C., these city dwellers were joined by traveling people known as the Aryans. These kingdoms moved into the Ganges River valley from western Asia.

For a long time after the Aryans arrived, India was made up of many small kingdoms. They were often at war.

After about A.D. 1000, soldiers from Afghanistan and Turkey began invading northern India. By about 1200, Muslim leaders called sultans ruled most of the Ganges River valley. They made their capital city at Delhi.

In 1526, Muslim invaders called Mughals arrived in the area. By 1530, they ruled most of northern India.

At about the same time the Mughals ruled, traders from Europe came to India. The Portuguese arrived first. Then came the Dutch and the British. India was rich in cotton cloth, silks, spices, and tea. European merchants took these goods back to Europe to sell at high prices.

Mughal rule was at its peak in 1700. After 1707, the power of the Mughals came to an end. India once again was divided into small kingdoms.

◄ *Afonso d'Albuquerque was a Portuguese general who went to India in the early 1500s.*

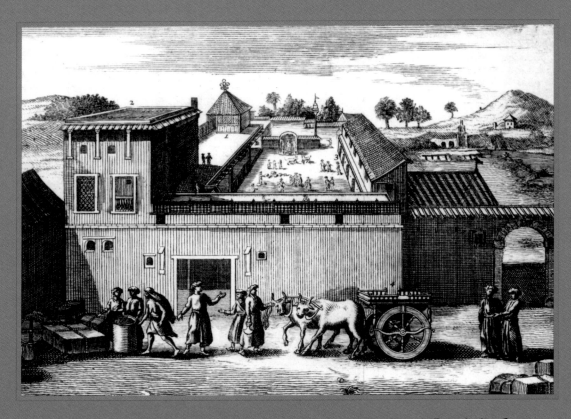

▲ *This trading post in Surat belonged to the British East India Company.*

In 1600, the British government allowed the British East India Company to settle and trade in India. Between 1757 and the 1840s, the company fought many long, bloody wars to gain control of India. In 1857, the Indian people rebelled. However, they did not win their independence.

In 1858, the British government took over control of India. After a century of fighting, India became an official part of the British **Empire.**

The Indian people did not like British rule. They wanted India to be an independent country. One of the leaders of the struggle for independence from the British Empire was Mohandas Gandhi. He taught people to protest British laws in a peaceful manner. The British were finally forced to leave. In 1947, India became an independent

◀ *Gandhi helped his country gain independence from Great Britain.*

country. The next year, Gandhi was killed by an Indian who didn't agree with his nonviolent beliefs. Gandhi's beliefs continue to influence people all over the world.

Today, India is known as the Republic of India. Its government is made up of a **parliament** elected by the people. Parliament members elect a president. The president chooses a prime minister. Both of them work with the parliament to run the country.

▲ *The Secretariat Buildings in New Delhi house many government offices.*

Made in India

Major manufacturing companies and other businesses exist in India. Factories produce fertilizer to help crops grow. Other factories process steel or make tools and machines. The growing electronics industry produces computers, televisions, and radios. India makes and launches its own **satellites.** The country also produces many motor vehicles.

India is the world's leading producer of tea and spices. Other important crops include rice, wheat, coffee, and sugarcane. India also mines iron ore and coal.

Many Indians are poor and live in the country. They use their crops

mostly to feed their own families. They use the products they make for their own needs, or they trade them for other items they may want.

▲ *Women in central India harvest rice.*

Life in India

More than 1,000 languages and **dialects** are spoken in India. The main language, however, is Hindi.

Most Indians are Hindus. Hinduism is one of the world's oldest religions. Hindus pray to many gods and goddesses. Other religions of India are Islam, Sikhism, and Jainism. There are also many Christians in India.

Indian society used to be divided into groups called castes. Priests and kings were in the

▲ *Two of the Hindu gods, Shiva and Parvati*

highest castes, and untouchables were in the lowest. Untouchables did dirty work such as handling garbage or human waste. The caste system, which was part of the Hindu religion, is now against the law in India. Many Indians still live and work within their caste, though.

Family life is important to the Indian people. In many homes, grandparents, parents, and children all live together.

▲ *Several generations often live in one house.*

▲ *A village in Kashmir*

Most of India's people live in small villages. Village homes are made of bamboo and palm leaves or mud, **dung,** and straw. Some homes are built on platforms to keep out floodwaters and snakes.

In the cities, people live in crowded apartment buildings. Many city dwellers are very poor and have no homes at all. They live in **slums.** Rich families in cities such as Mumbai, Calcutta, and Delhi live in large homes with electricity, toilets, and clean water.

▲ *Poorer families often live in crowded apartments like these.*

Indian children between the ages of six and fourteen are supposed to attend school. They study grammar, spelling, math, and science. They also take classes in social studies, English, art, and physical education. Most

▲ *Students in India study many of the same subjects as children in the United States.*

students go to school through the tenth grade. Students who plan to go to college stay through the twelfth grade and must pass a difficult exam.

Only half of Indian children over the age of ten attend school, however. Many children must work to help earn money for their families.

After school and work, Indians like to have fun. Children play sports or cards with friends. Older students go out together in groups. They go to the movies or watch television.

Indians of all ages enjoy games of skill. It is believed that chess began in India more than 1,000 years ago. The British brought the sport of cricket to India. It is India's most popular sport. Indians also enjoy field hockey, badminton, soccer, volleyball, and polo.

▲ In India, cricket attracts players of all ages.

Festivals and Holidays

There is a festival somewhere in India almost every day. Each small village has its own special day of celebration. In addition to these, big festivals and holidays are celebrated all over the country.

Many festivals are part of the Hindu religion. Diwali is the Hindu New Year. It comes at the end of October or the beginning of November. Diwali lasts for five days. People exchange presents and dress up.

▲ *A Calcutta marketplace is lit up to celebrate Diwali.*

▲ *The sprinkling of colored water and powder on Holi is meant to ward off evil spirits.*

Holi is also a Hindu festival. Held in February or March, Holi celebrates the arrival of spring. During Holi, people splash each other with brightly colored water and powder. Hindus believe the bright colors scare away evil spirits.

In southern India, Hindus celebrate Pongal. This festival is held at the end of winter. Children celebrate Pongal by flying kites.

India has two national holidays. Independence Day is August 15. It honors the day India became independent from Great Britian. Republic Day is January 26. It marks the day the Republic of India was founded. Parades are held throughout India on Republic Day.

▲ *Floats in a Republic Day parade*

▲ *India celebrates many of its holidays with festive parades.*

Arts and Literature

Indian arts and crafts date back thousands of years. In cities, towns, and villages, people create beautiful pottery. Other traditional crafts include basket making, woodcarving, and metalworking.

▲ *This Indian craftsperson carefully works on a bronze sculpture.*

▲ *A silk sari shop at Kanchipuram*

India is well known for its silk and cotton cloth. Plaid cotton fabric called madras is named for the Indian city where it was first made. That city is now called Chennai. Tie-dyeing is the art of making colorful patterns by tying fabric with string and dipping it in dyes. Tie-dyeing is an ancient art in India.

▲ *An Orissa girl performing one of the oldest classical dances*

There are two kinds of Indian dance—classical and folk. There are six types of classical dance. It takes years of practice to perform these dances well. Folk dancing is a less structured kind of dance. Folk dancers perform at most festivals.

Throughout India, many temples are more than 1,000 years old. A temple is a building used for worship. Temples are decorated with paintings and sculptures of plants, animals, and gods. In southern India, bronze statues of Hindu gods decorate the temples.

▲ *A statue of Buddha in a Hindu monastery*

The most famous building in India is the Taj Mahal. It was built by Shah Jahan as a burial place for his wife, Mumtaz Mahal. It is located on the Yamuna River near Agra and took eleven years to build (from 1632 to 1643). People from all over the world come to India to see the huge Taj Mahal. Its name means "Crown Palace."

◄ *The historic Taj Mahal is more than three hundred years old.*

Fine works of literature have been written in nearly every one of India's many languages. Each state in the country of India has its own official language.

The oldest Indian writings are Hindu hymns and chants called the Vedas. The Upanishads are religious lessons found in the Vedas. For many years, the Vedas were told from one generation to the next. Later they were written in Sanskrit, one of the world's oldest languages.

Great Indian poets include Mirza Ghalib and Sarojini Naidu. Rabindranath Tagore wrote spiritual poetry about religion and the beauty of the earth. He received the Nobel Prize for Literature in 1913.

Famous Indian stories include the Puranas (poo-RA-nahs) and the Panchatantra (PAANCH-ah-TAAN-tra). The Puranas tell stories about Hinduism and teachings from the Vedas. The Panchatantra are Buddhist stories that use human and animal characters to teach people about right and wrong.

▲ Poet and Nobel Prize winner Rabindranath Tagore

Indian Food

▲ *A variety of spices are sold at Indian markets.*

Indian food has many spices. Some Indian spices are mild, and others are very hot. Saffron, cumin, and cinnamon are the most common. Curry powder, a combination of several spices, is also common.

The most impor-tant foods in India are wheat, rice, and lentils. Chapati is a common wheat bread. Round and flat, it looks like a tortilla. Another round, flat bread is called nan. Nutty-smelling rice is called basmati. Basmati rice is served with many different types of dishes. Lentils are used in a stew called dal.

◄ *A baker prepares bread for a restaurant in Calcutta.*

▲ *Indian food is sometimes served on a banana leaf.*

The usual Indian lunch or dinner is one or two vegetables cooked in oil and spices. They are served with lentils, yogurt, and rice or chapatis. *Paratha* (puh-RAH-tha) is eaten on special occasions. Parathas look like chapatis. They are fried and stuffed with meat or vegetables. Sometimes they are fried with an egg on top.

Indians enjoy desserts. Two favorites are spiced rice pudding and an ice cream called *kulfi*. During religious festivals, sweets made with milk, nuts, and dried fruit are also popular.

Indian Clothing

Most traditional clothing in India is made of cotton. In villages, men wear dhotis (DOE-tees). A dhoti is a long, white cloth. It wraps around the waist and

between the legs. In southern India, some men wear long, wrap-around skirts called *lungis* (LUNE-ghees). In large towns and cities, men wear Western-style clothing. They wear suits to work and jeans while relaxing.

◄ *Indian men and women traditionally wear dhotis and saris.*

△ *This woman wears a beautifully decorated sari.*

In villages as well as big cities, most women wear saris (SAR-ees). They are long strips of colorful cloth that are wrapped around the body. One end forms a skirt. The other end becomes a covering for the head or shoulders. Some northern Indian women wear long pants, a tunic, and a scarf. These outfits are called Punjabi suits.

Throughout India, some children wear traditional clothes. Many boys, however, wear jeans and T-shirts. Girls wear skirts and blouses. Schoolchildren wear uniforms.

Some Indians wear clothing based on their religion. Men who practice Sikhism wear head coverings called turbans. Some women who practice Islam wear hooded cloaks called burkas.

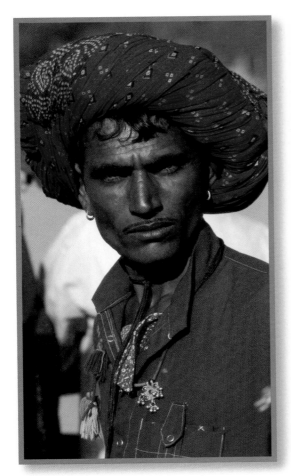 

▲ *Turbans (left) and burkas (right) are two examples of clothing influenced by religious beliefs in India.*

India Today

India has a rich history and culture. Over the years, it has struggled to improve the lives of its citizens. The country has made much progress.

India is the largest **democracy** in the world. Like Americans, Indians value their personal freedoms. Those freedoms are leading many Indians to start their own businesses. Others seek to improve India through **technology.** These and other improvements have helped make India a major Asian nation. As life continues to get better for all Indians, the country is taking its place as one of the leading nations of the world.

▲ *Improved technology and new businesses have made India an important nation and a better place to live.*

Glossary

democracy—a way of governing a country in which the people choose their leaders in elections

dialects—forms of speech spoken in a certain area or by a certain group of people

dung—the solid waste of animals

empire—a group of countries under one ruler or government, with one country having control over the rest

parliament—a group of people who are elected to make laws

peninsula—a piece of land that sticks out from a larger landmass and is almost completely surrounded by water

satellites—spacecraft sent into orbit around Earth or the Moon

slums—overcrowded, poor, and neglected areas of housing in a town or city

technology—the use of science and engineering to accomplish practical things

Did You Know?

- The Himalayas contain the highest peaks in the world.

- Gandhi's followers called him Mahatma, meaning "great soul."

- More movies are made in India each year than in any other country.

At a Glance

Official name: Republic of India

Capital: New Delhi

Official languages: Hindi is the national language, and English is an associate national language. Each state within India has its own official language.

National song: "Jana-Gana-Mana" ("Thou Art the Ruler of All Minds of All People")

Area: 1,269,346 square miles (3,287,606 square kilometers)

Highest point: Kanchenjunga, 28,208 feet (8,603 meters)

Lowest point: Sea level along the coast

Population: 1,045,845,200 (2002 estimate)

Head of government: Prime minister

Money: Indian rupee

Important Dates

2500 B.C.	In what later becomes India, the earliest civilizations begin along the Indus River.
1500 B.C.	Aryans from Asia move into northern India.
A.D. 1000	Soldiers from Afghanistan and Turkey invade what is now India.
1200	Leaders called sultans rule northern India.
1526	Mughals invade India.
1530	Mughals rule northern India; the first European traders arrive.
1707	Mughal rule in India begins to weaken rapidly.
1858	Control of India is taken from the British East India Company, and India is ruled directly by the British monarch.
1869	Mohandas Gandhi is born in the Indian state of Gujarat.
1947	India becomes an independent country.
1948	Gandhi is killed.
1966	Indira Gandhi becomes India's first woman prime minister.
1996	A group of political parties rules India.

Want to Know More?

At the Library

Hill, Valerie, and Judith Simpson. *India.* Broomall, Pa.: Mason Crest, 2002.

McCulloch, Julie. *India.* Des Plaines, Ill.: Heinemann Library, 2001.

Pluckrose, Henry. *India.* Danbury, Conn.: Franklin Watts, 1998.

On the Web

Discover India—Holidays and Festivals
http://www.indonet.com/HolidaysandFestivals.html
For descriptions of Indian holidays and religious festivals

Indianvisit
http://www.indianvisit.com/india
For information about India's environment, a map, and links to the country's sights and attractions

Through the Mail
Embassy of India in the United States
2107 Massachusetts Avenue, N.W.
Washington, DC 20008
202/939-7000
To learn more about India and to plan a trip

On the Road
Indian American Cultural Association
1281 Cooper Lake Road S.E.
Smyrna, GA 30082
To learn about the history and contributions of the Indian people in America

Afghanistan, 10
British East India Company, 12
Buddhism, 34
Calcutta, 6, 21
caste system, 18–19
chess, 23
children, 22, 25, 40
classical dance, 30
clothing, 39–41
cricket, 23
Delhi, 10, 21
families, 19, 22
farming, 8, 9, 16–17
festivals, 24, 25
folk dance, 30
foods, 36–38
Gandhi, Mohandas, 13–14
government, 6, 10, 14, 42
Great Britain, 11, 12–13, 23
Himalaya Mountains, 7
Hindi language, 4, 18
Hinduism, 18, 19, 24, 25, 31
holidays, 24, 26
housing, 20, 21

independence, 12, 13
kingdoms, 10, 11
languages, 4, 18, 34
literature, 34
madras (fabric), 29
manufacturing, 16
Mughals, 10, 11
Mumbai, 6, 21
North Indian Plain, 8, 9
parliament, 14
peninsula, 5, 7
presidents, 14
religion, 18, 30–31, 41
rivers, 8
schools, 22
slums, 21
spices, 11, 16, 36, 38
sports, 23
sultans, 10
Taj Mahal, 33
temples, 30–31
Thar Desert, 9
tie-dyeing, 29
weather, 7, 8–9

About the Author

Sarah E. De Capua enjoys writing about other countries. Researching the manuscripts gives her a chance to read many other books about those countries. Reading good books about faraway places can be a way to visit them!

When she is not working as an author and editor of children's books, De Capua enjoys traveling from her home in Colorado to places she has written about, as well as to places she may write about in the future.